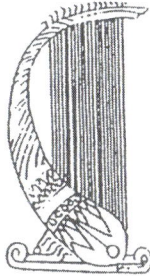

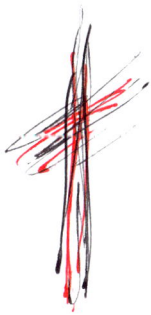

**WATCH THE
QR VIDEO
ON PAGE 50**

THE LEGEND OF
DAVID'S
AMAZING
HARP

DAVID M. HARRISON

Address all personal correspondence to:
David Harrison
P.O. Box 3021
Chattanooga, Tennessee 37404

Individuals and church groups may order books from David Harrison directly, or from the publisher. Retailers and wholesalers should order from our distributors. Refer to the Deeper Revelation Books website for distribution information, as well as an online catalog of all our books.

Published by:
Deeper Revelation Books
Revealing "the deep things of God" (1 Cor. 2:10)
P.O. Box 4260, Cleveland, TN 37320 423-478-2843
Website: www.deeperrevelationbooks.org
Email: info@deeperrevelationbooks.org

Deeper Revelation Books assist Christian authors in publishing and distributing their books. Final responsibility for design, content, permissions, editorial accuracy, and doctrinal views, either expressed or implied, belongs to the author. We consider it a great honor and blessing to collaborate in projects intended to advance the kingdom of God.

The Legend of David's Amazing Harp is fiction based on a vision of the author. No biblical or historical facts support that this story actually happened in David's life as a sheep herder. However, this biblical fiction story could be plausible. Let it warm your heart and life.

Testimonies

"Thank you for sharing *The Legend of David's Amazing Harp* with me. It was beautifully done and touched my heart. I have read some parts over again and planned to read it again and again. Bless you."

— Ruby B., Nebraska

"*The Legend of David's Amazing Harp* is a precious, heartfelt story. When I finished, I was totally moved by it."

— Marlene L., Minnesota

"I enjoyed the Harp book and learned a lot about harps and David's other instruments and how they were used. The book was a blessing to me in its overall message."

— Doreen S., Florida

"Thank you for the lovely book, *The Legend of David's Amazing Harp.* I enjoyed reading it so much."

— Lili Anne P., Maryland

Testimonies – continued

"I loved the story of *The Legend of David's Amazing Harp*. After reading it several times, I decided to read the story to the children in Junior Church. Well done, brother."

— David C., Chattanooga, Tennessee

"Please send me a dozen copies of *The Legend of David's Amazing Harp*. It is a beautiful story. I was impressed with the way you wrote it."

— Ruth H., Lynchburg, Virginia

"Thank you for the beautiful book you wrote."

— Ben H., Virginia

"Dear Cathy and Dave, Thanks so much for the little book you wrote and self-published. It really looks professional and reads well."

— Leilani M., Texas

"Thank you for your fascinating book."

— Ramona B., North Dakota

"Thanks for the booklet. You folks have a lot of talent."

— Jennie T., Illinois

Testimonies – continued

"I enjoyed Dave's booklet! Thank you so much for sharing with me."

— Mary C., Virginia

"I liked the Twenty-Third Psalm book. It was good of you to send it."

— Lois D., Michigan

"Thank you for the wonderful booklet. You are both talented writers!"

— Darlene R., Washington

"Thank you so much for the beautiful book. Patrick lost his dad this past summer, and *The Legend of David's Amazing Harp* was a great read to comfort the soul."

— Tracy C., Missionaries to Ireland

"Thank you, David, for your beautiful book. It is indeed a labor of love. It has deeply touched my heart to be a recipient of such a fine gift. My deaf mother passed away on December 27. She is listening to David play his Amazing Harp. May God bless you."

— Bonnie, K., Chattanooga, Tennessee

Testimonies – continued

"So I sat here this morning, my husband's funeral day, dreading it more than any other day in my life. I remembered the little booklet you handed me at the funeral home. What a comfort this story became as I read David Harrison's spirit-filled composition. This story really met a need in my heart this morning. Thank you for sharing it with me."

— Joyce W., Tennessee

"Thank you for the booklet, *The Legend of David's Amazing Harp*. I enjoyed reading it."

— Ruth W., B.C., Canada

"Thank you for the story, *The Legend of David's Amazing Harp*. I've sometimes felt, too, that God speaks through nature. There's a lot of peace in those bright, cold, snowy nights, and I'm confident He designed it that way."

— Dr. Linda E., Wisconsin

"The book, *The Legend of David's Amazing Harp*, will be especially cherished. Thanks."

— Bethany R., Alabama

Testimonies – continued

"Wonderful, absolutely wonderful! I have read it several times, and I plan to reread it. It really blessed my soul. I keep your book with my Bible."

— Organist Fred. R. Jr.

"My friend, Bill, and his wife were most impressed with your presentation of *The Legend of David's Amazing Harp*. Your booklet struck a chord with me (pun intended). *The Legend of David's Amazing Harp* really meant a lot."

— McMillion, Chattanooga

Dedication

It gives me great pleasure to honor and dedicate this story to my twin brother, Donald E. Harrison (right). He was a good brother to me!

Dedication – continued

To my dear precious wife, Cathy Hart, thank you in helping me put this story together. I miss you every day and look forward to our heavenly reunion.

My greatest gratitude goes to my heavenly Father, His Son, and the Holy Spirit—whose story has touched my heart for time and eternity.

Table of Contents

.

Introduction

You are about to read a fictional story of a harp that young David built while tending sheep. This one harp brought peace of mind and comfort to many people. Nothing soothes the restless soul more quickly than the soft music of a harp. This beautiful instrument brings contentment to the sad at heart and lifts the spirits of those who mourn. The world needs comfort during times of grief, disappointment, sorrow, and suffering. Music has always been an encouragement when the heart is heavy. Reading the Psalms or other passages from the Bible brings comfort. I believe the greatest passage ever written is David's Psalm 23. This Psalm has blessed many hearts with great comfort and peace.

God inspired *The Legend of David's Amazing Harp* while I was getting ready to attend my brother's funeral. We all have or will experience the loss of someone we deeply love. It is during those times that we must rely on God's peace and strength. It was through this event that I gained an appreciation for the story of David and how his love of music brought peace to situations (Psalm 91:1).

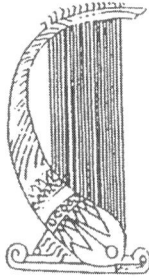

CHAPTER 1

My Birthday

It was Saturday, July 10, 1999, my birthday. The family was planning a special day for me. Shortly after breakfast, I began to get a headache. The pain started on my forehead and then moved around to my back, increasing in severity. My eyes became sensitive to light and noise, and the pain was unbearable. It felt like the worst migraine anyone could ever experience. All I could do was suffer in a dark room.

At 5 p.m. the telephone rang. It was my sister from Minnesota calling. Her words were serious. She said, "Your twin brother is in the hospital at Sioux Falls, South Dakota, and had to have a large tumor removed from his brain. The doctors are saying he has six months to live."

I was shocked! The last I had heard from Don, he was living and teaching at a university in South Korea. "What was he doing in the States?" I asked her.

My mind went crazy with questions, and I had no answers. I just knew my brother had a tumor removed. I thought that with my headache as bad as it was, I, too, must have a tumor, and my time was also limited. That must be why I was having a headache.

Did you know identical twins sometimes experience sympathy pain for one another even if they are miles apart? I was experiencing this type of pain and had felt the entire operation of my brother, just as I once had when my brother had eye surgery when he was in Germany.

As my headache began to ease and thinking my life was ending, I went to my office to pray. I anxiously opened my Bible looking for answers to the situation I was facing.

Psalm 91

The Lord directed me to Psalm 91:

He that dwelleth in the secret place of the most High shall abide under the shadow of the Almighty. I will say of the LORD, He is my refuge and my fortress: my God; in him will I trust. Surely he shall deliver thee from the snare of the fowler, and from the noisome pestilence. He shall cover thee with his feathers, and under his wings shalt thou trust: his truth shall be thy shield and buckler. Thou shalt not be afraid for the terror by night; nor for the arrow that flieth by day; Nor for the pestilence that walketh in darkness; nor for the destruction that wasteth at noonday. A thousand shall fall at thy side, and ten thousand at thy right hand; but it shall not come nigh thee. Only with thine eyes shalt thou behold and see the reward of the wicked. Because thou hast made the LORD, which is my refuge, even the most High, thy habitation; There shall no evil befall thee, neither shall any plague come nigh thy dwelling. For he shall give his angels charge over thee, to keep thee in all thy ways. They shall bear thee up in their hands, lest thou dash thy foot against a stone. Thou shalt tread upon the lion and adder: the young lion and the dragon shalt thou trample under feet. Because he hath set his love upon me, therefore will I deliver him: I will set him on high, because he hath known my name. He shall call upon me, and I will answer him: I will be with him in trouble; I will deliver him, and honour him. With long life will I satisfy him, and shew him my salvation.

God always blesses the one who spends time in the secret place of prayer. David declares a list of powerful promises to those who abide and live separated from the world and in a personal relationship with the God of the universe. There is power no foe can withstand. The God of heaven breaks in here and affirms all the promises spoken by King David.

Here is my translation of those verses:

Because you (David) have set your love upon Me, therefore I (the Lord) will deliver you: I will set you on high because you know My name. You shall call upon Me when you pray, and I will answer you. I will be with you in trouble; I, the Lord, will honor you. With long life will I satisfy you and show you My great salvation.

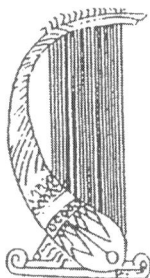

CHAPTER 2

My Brother Don

Donald Harrison was my twin brother (he was born fifteen minutes after me). We were both born in Mountain View, Minnesota, and grew up in St. Paul. Growing up, my brother got into trouble with a gang and broke into a liquor store. The judge gave each member of the gang a choice to get involved with a church or join the Army. Don decided to drop out of high school and join the paratroopers.

While he was serving in Germany, an Army chaplain named Merlin Carothers (a former bodyguard for General Dwight D. Eisenhower), came to the base to share the gospel. After hearing the Word of God ministered over several nights, Don fell under great conviction and surrendered his life to Jesus Christ.

After his salvation, he immediately transformed his life. He quit smoking and drinking, changed his language, and burned his pornographic magazines.

He took his salvation seriously and loved to read and study God's Word. Because of this, Jesus transformed his life. Once he left the Army, he attended Luther Rice Seminary and earned his Doctor of Ministry degree. He taught at Liberty University in Lynchburg, Virginia, for seventeen years. Then he moved to South Korea and taught there until he returned to the States for his surgery.

Don was a true lover of God, and he faithfully served Him right up to the day he passed away. He was always thankful for the opportunity the judge had given him so many years ago and for the chaplain who selflessly shared the gospel with him.

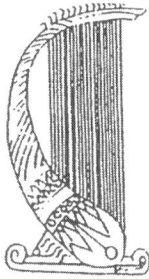

CHAPTER 3

The Funeral

My brother Don passed into the presence of the Lord on December 16, 1999. The funeral was set for Monday, December 20, 1999. The temperature outside had dropped, and the estimated temperature was forty-five degrees below zero with the wind chill.

Flying from Chattanooga to St. Paul was no easy feat in the peak of the Christmas season. I am very thankful to the Lord and some dear friends for making it possible.

The day before the funeral, I was struggling with the loss of my brother. I was sad and asking God for peace. Everyone knows it is hard to deal with the death of a loved one. I had some doubts and anxious moments as to why all this was happening. Why did my brother's life end so early? Would mine as well? I had a lot of questions I had no answers to.

I retired to my room Sunday evening. A full moon shone, and I could hear the wind blowing as I rested.

I awoke at 5 a.m. and decided to go for a long walk. Fresh snow had fallen during the night, and the air was very crisp. The blanket of snow sparkled and glowed with a pure angelic white everywhere. As I waded through the fluffy white layer of snow, the sound of each step would squeak as my foot hit the ground. The morning beauty was so overwhelming and soothing as I hiked along the pristine wooded area. The walk was so beautiful, peaceful, and still.

My heart was heavy with sadness as I prayed and meditated on the message God wanted me to give for the funeral. I began to experience an epiphany, a sudden and striking realization or revelation. I sensed the presence of God, and I felt and heard the sound of beautiful harp music and singing. It seemed the music was coming from above me, and yet I could experience the music within my heart.

As I focused on the inner music, the story of *The Legend of David's Amazing Harp* unfolded before me. Great peace flooded my soul, and the tranquil surroundings heightened the joy of it all. My heart shouted out to God in thanksgiving for the beautiful gift of such sweet peace. What was the Lord saying to me personally? He was saying His presence of peace is like the beautiful music of a harp and His healing power was there to comfort my heart.

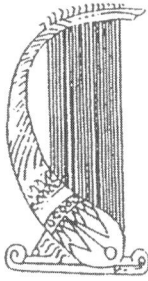

CHAPTER 4

The Legend of David's Amazing Harp

David, the shepherd boy, was an industrious and ingenious worker, as well as a superb sheepherder. Young David used his time wisely, learning how to use a sling with either hand and how to make tools, weapons, and instruments for entertainment.

In those days, men made their tools, weapons, and instruments for entertainment. The most widely used device was a flute carved from a hollow reed. However, a person could not sing and play the pipe at the same time.

One day, an Egyptian caravan or camel train traveling through the Jordan Rift Valley set up camp nearby for water and rest. Young David became intrigued when he heard music coming from the camp. He had to find out what made that beautiful music. He had never heard harp music; in fact, harps were very rare for centuries.

As David drew close to the camp, he met an old Egyptian man who had a magnificent harp. I believe that the Egyptian man was a theophany, a visitation from God on a special mission to give an individual instruction of great importance.

The Egyptian traveler told David that the harp was a unique instrument already patterned in heaven. He shared heaven's blueprint and taught David how to produce this unique instrument. He told David to look for a specific type of gourd that grew in ravines near the desert. With the gourd as the harp's base, David would then have to make the strings and mount them. The traveler spent a lot of time sharing the details of making the harp and giving him lessons in how to play it, along with singing lessons.

One day while herding his sheep from the desert to a ravine for water and rest, David noticed a vine hanging from a cliff. Among the gourds hanging on the vine, one gourd caught his eye. It was the most enormous gourd he had ever seen, and the convex shape or vertical section seemed perfect for building his harp.

The gourd sounded hollow and felt dry and very hard. David felt that this gourd would be large and hollow enough to attach strings and amplify thc music. So, David gathered the gourd and began to build the harp of his dream. I believe the Lord helped him build it to perfection.

David tried to remember everything the traveler shared with him and relied on God to help him build it perfectly. There were so many details like how many holes to drill and cut, how many strings to make (strings were made from animal guts), how to create the wrest (or peg) blocks, and even how to decorate it with ornaments. It would prove a long, tedious task.

Finally, after David had attached the strings correctly, tightened them with the pegs to create the right pitch, and stained and polished this fantastic instrument, he was able to play his new harp.

This harp was the first of more than 4,000 instruments built in his lifetime: "Moreover four thousand were porters; and four thousand praised the LORD with the instruments which I made, said David, to praise therewith" (1 Chronicles 23:5).

David had designed his own harp. He was eager to learn to play his own unique invention, would practice for hours while the sheep grazed peacefully. After many hours and days, he finally mastered playing his harp.

The music flowed from his harp with soothing beauty. His harp produced a solemn or a grave sound that had a natural tendency to compose and calm the mind, heart, and soul. It brought such peace and comfort to everyone who heard it. Shepherds and travelers came from all over Israel to hear David's amazing harp. Under the light of the moon, sweet music flowed down the hillside and ascended to the heavens. David declared, "I will sing a new song unto thee, O God: upon a psaltery and an instrument of ten strings will I sing praise unto thee" (Psalm 144:9).

His talent was undisputed in all the land. One day, David was called in from the sheep field and was secretly anointed king by the prophet Samuel. At that moment, the Holy Spirit came upon David, while the Spirit departed from King Saul (1 Samuel 16:12–13).

Saul, who reigned on the throne, had received an evil spirit that troubled him (1 Samuel 16:14). The king grew fretful, discontented, vindictive, and suspicious. The soul of King Saul was so troubled and miserable that he begged for something or someone to bring peace to his heart. He said, "Provide me now a man that can play [a harp] well, and bring him to me" (1 Samuel 16:17).

The servants of the palace told King Saul of a shepherd boy who played the harp with such skill and beauty that even evil spirits would flee. The son of Jesse was genuinely anointed of God and played heavenly music on his harp. David was summoned to appear before the king to play his harp.

Sitting before the king, David began to play as never before on his amazing harp. When he played, all activities ceased in the palace. In fact, the entire city stood still just to hear this beautiful angelic music. Later the king felt refreshed and well from his troubles as the evil spirits departed from him (1 Samuel 16:23).

Skill in anything comes from much practice. David possessed musical abilities far beyond his age, and his nimble fingers moved with grace and swiftness. Just to watch the movement of his hands amazed those who observed them. He was doing what seemed impossible on a home-crafted instrument. David would tell you that his musicianship came from the Lord God Almighty.

When David's brothers were called to serve in Saul's army, he returned to his sheep near Bethlehem. He began to ponder how people go through a long, dark valley of death and despair. He thought about all the troubles that plagued humanity everywhere: sin, tension, strife, restlessness, greed, anxiety, war, and fighting all around the land. All the money, power, and possessions in the world could not satisfy the heart or bring peace to the soul. There must be something or someone that could bring peace to people of all nationalities of life.

David thought and prayed for a long time about the troubles in the land. "What could I give?" he pondered. "If it were in my power, I would offer one of my sons to bring forgiveness of sin and lasting peace to the world."

One night when David's heart was so filled with the love of God, he began to play on his harp. Camped on a hill called Moriah, David noticed the night air seemed so clear and the stars unusually bright. He was searching for a message of hope to give to the world.

All the angels of heaven ceased their activities and gathered around the hill outside of Bethlehem just to hear David sing and play his harp. The angels wept with joy because mankind was so troubled and needed such comfort. The song David sang that night touched and moved the very heart of God. The singing voice of David was so tender, pure, and melodious. He began to sing the words of the most beautiful psalm ever known to man. Whether the psalm was read, quoted from memory, sung, or accompanied by music, it had the same soothing effect on the heart, mind, and soul.

Listen to David's song as he introduces the world to Israel's shepherd, who became the sacrificial "Lamb of God," slain from the foundation of the world. David wanted everyone to know the "Prince of Peace."

The angels knew that they would return to this very hill to announce the birth of the Son of God, who was the seed of David. God's Lamb would take away the sins of the world and bring great peace to man. The angels would give their message to a group of lowly shepherds like David:

> *"Fear not: for, behold, I bring you good tidings of great joy, which shall be to all people. For unto you is born this day in the city of David a Saviour, which is Christ the Lord. And this shall be a sign*

unto you; Ye shall find the babe wrapped in swaddling clothes, lying in a manger. And suddenly there was with the angel a multitude of the heavenly host praising God, and saying, Glory to God in the highest, and on earth peace, good will toward men" (Luke 2:10–14).

David did not know that among his descendants, one would be anointed the Messiah, Jesus Christ, the son of David, chosen by God to take away our sins and bring true peace and eternal salvation. Christ is referred to nine times in the Gospel of Matthew as the "Son of David" (Matthew 1:1, 9:27, 12:23, 15:22, 20:30–31, 21:9–15, 22:42). David didn't know his song, Psalm 23, would be a message of peace to the world. No music as beautiful as David's has been heard on earth again. Only those who have accepted Christ the Messiah into their hearts and lives will listen to David's music when they enter heaven.

I believe every believer will be greeted with love and jubilation by a large group of heavenly hosts, perhaps like the group at the birth announcement of Christ. Your loved ones and families will be united again to spend eternity rejoicing and praising the Lord forever. Oh, what a great day that will be. Great peace and comfort will flood your soul.

Revelation 14:2 tells us that we will listen to the singing voices of "harpers harping with their harps." Picture 144,000 men singing a new song that sounds like thunder, and each one will have a beautiful grand harp, the same type of harp David learned how to build from the old Egyptian traveler.

In conclusion, I believe that there will be a beautiful memorial garden somewhere in heaven to commemorate many great events and notable objects in biblical history: the burning bush, Moses's rod, Elijah's mantel, the tabernacle, the Ten Commandments, Solomon's temple, Noah's ark, and the upper room, to name a few things. Somewhere in this beautiful garden, I think we will find a large block of gold with David's immortal words of Psalm 23 engraved with many colorful pearls. And hanging on the side of this magnificent memorial, you will find David's Amazing Harp.

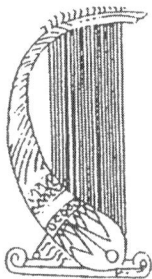

Psalm 23

The LORD is my shepherd; I shall not want.

He maketh me to lie down in green pastures: he leadeth me beside the still waters.

He restoreth my soul: he leadeth me in the paths of righteousness for his name's sake.

Yea, though I walk through the valley of the shadow of death, I will fear no evil: for thou art with me; thy rod and thy staff they comfort me.

Thou preparest a table before me in the presence of mine enemies: thou anointest my head with oil; my cup runneth over.

Surely goodness and mercy shall follow me all the days of my life: and I will dwell in the house of the LORD for ever.

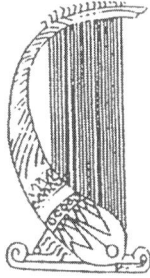

CHAPTER 5

Melodies and Music

What are melodies?

Melodies are the part of music above the chords and rhythm. They come in many shapes and sizes and can have lyrics or be solely instrumental. They can be played very high or very low. We can hear them played by instruments like a violin, guitar, saxophone, or trumpet or sung by a voice.

The oldest musical composition to have survived in its entirety is a first-century Greek tune known as the "Seikilos Epitaph." The song was found engraved on an ancient marble column used to mark a woman's gravesite in Turkey.

The ancient Greek word for melody was *melodia*, used to denote a tune for lyric poetry. It was derived from *melos,* which meant "song." In most songs, the melody follows a logical pattern that creates a memorable line of notes. The vocal melody was written to be sung by a human voice. Consider

Psalms like 41, 42, 44, 45, 47, etc. The harp was strummed lightly by a plectrum (or a pick) only to accompany vocal melodies. The music touched the heart and calmed the soul.

How were melodies invented?

No one really knows who invented music. No historical evidence exists to tell us exactly who sang the first song or created the first rhythmic sounds that resemble what we know today as music. However, Genesis 4:21 tells us that the first musician was Jubal, the son of Lamech: "... he was the father of all such as handle the harp and organ." He is described as the "the father of all who play stringed instruments and pipes" (paraphrased). He was the one who created music that was played on instruments.

The oldest musical instruments in the world are thought to be wind instruments. The flutes were the oldest instrument family that was made in the Upper Paleolithic age and are more commonly accepted as being the oldest known musical instruments. Archaeological evidence of musical instruments was discovered in excavations at the Royal Cemetery in the Sumerian city of Ur.

Although flutes are instruments held by the musician, early human ancestors may have used their hands for clapping to create rhythmic music. The Israelite women, led by Miriam, displayed the first rhythmic music after they crossed the Red Sea in victory. This victory is probably gave them the idea to develop percussion by banging sticks and stones together to create sounds.

The timbrel or tabret (also known as the *tof* for the ancient Hebrews, the *deff* for Muslims, and the *adufe* for the Spanish Moors) was the principal percussion instrument of the ancient Israelites. It was a circular instrument made of wood with metal discs attached to it and resembled either a frame drum or a modern tambourine. The timbrel was developed in Egypt and was later played by the Israelite women after the Egyptian army drowned in the Red Sea.

The name "tambourine" (also called "trimble") comes from the section of Exodus 15 known in Hebrew as *Shirat Hayam* (Song of the Sea) or *Shirat Miriam* (Song of Miriam). It includes this verse: "And Miriam the prophetess, the sister of Aaron, took a timbrel in her hand; and all the women went out after her with timbrels and with dances" (Exodus 15:20). Today we use the generic word "drum" for timbrel.

The term "drum" signifies an instrument (such as a flute) which was combined with the timbrel drum and the harp (the national instrument of the Hebrews) because the latter was considered to be a joyful instrument.

The word "timbrel" is used in the Hebrew Bible in both its singular and plural forms. The singular form refers to a hoop of wood or metal over which a parchment head was stretched; the plural form perhaps designates a tambourine with bells or jangles fixed at intervals in hoops.

My dad and his homespun music

Growing up in Southern Minnesota, we children discovered many ways to make types of music. On the farm we had empty oil drums or milk pails to bang on or to holler in to create some sort of music. We had an urge to make music (well, at least what we thought of as music). It was in our blood.

My father, John Harrison, created a country band called Whoopee John's Band. He chose the name Whoopee John as he would memorize songs for square dance calls and poems for entertainment. He said that members in his band would play the fiddle, castanets made with two spoons taped together, a washtub base fiddle, and a galvanized corrugated washboard. I never heard his band play in the early '20s and '30s. But his love to create music at home from household items amazed my family.

He would set up several wine glasses and fill them with water at different levels. Dipping his finger in the water, he would begin rubbing the rim of the glasses to create different tones. One day he decided to try something new, so he set up several wine bottles and filled them with water at different levels. Then he blew across the top of the bottles creating homemade music. He would sometimes pull out his saw from the workbench and would hold it with his knees. Then he would bend the saw. He would then take a spoon and tap it on the saw, creating different melodies for our entertainment. Later, he bought a violin bow and was able to play beautiful music on the back side of the saw.

When he got a guitar, he would strum the strings and slide a steel bar, such as a knife handle, and create a Hawaiian sound. He loved to cup his hands together and whistle. With a blade of grass held between his thumbs, he could blow on the blade to make a whistle sound. Part of his singing included yodeling, which he learned from Swiss and cowboy singers. My dad was very musical. He loved creating and playing all types of music.

"Let Me Hear Your Harp"

© 2020 by David Harrison

I heard the harps of God

when my heart was grieving

sweet music from heaven

comforted my soul with joy

> *Once more, let me hear*
> *David's Amazing Harp*

My heart was troubled

filled with worry and fear

then the harp of heaven

restored my faith in God

> *Once more, let me hear*
> *David's Amazing Harp*

Life felt lonely and empty

with no one to turn to.

Prayer was my last hope

God answered by His music

> *Once more, let me hear*
> *David's Amazing Harp*

Pain and trials disappeared

when I sought the Lord

with my whole heart and soul

Blessings flowed from the harp

> *Once more, let me hear*
> *David's Amazing Harp*

Oh, to hear that celestial harp

that calms the spirit and soul

let the peace of God begin its

work of love in me again

> *Once more, let me hear*
> *David's Amazing Harp*

Deaf ears cannot hear God's harp

but I know there will be scores of

harpers playing on harps in heaven

welcoming me with a victory song

> *With joy, I will now hear*
> *David's Amazing Harp again.*

Letter of Invitation

Many people were healed and relieved of evil spirits under the music of David's Amazing Harp. The Psalms today still have their soothing effect. Through the Psalms of David, we can experience comfort, love, strength, and blessings untold. Above all, we find forgiveness of sin and deliverance from the evil plaguing the human heart today.

Sin causes so many diseases and ailments to the body. Much sickness may not be physical but rather psychosomatic. Most of our physical problems are triggered by guilt, fear, hate, anxiety, distrust, and even unbelief. When we are restless and disturbed, we have no peace in our souls.

When guilt dominates our minds, we tend to be irrational in our behavior. We tend to hide our sin deep within our soul. Sooner or later, it expresses itself in many ways, such as anger, violence, murder, or even suicide. It can drive us to alcohol, drugs, or other such addictive practices.

We do not know how to deal with these frustrations, so we bury them in all kinds of things such as sports, TV, parties, or loud music. We do not like to be reminded that sin is the root cause of most of our problems. We want to consider ourselves good and refuse to admit we are guilty of any sin. Hidden sin has a nasty way of coming out in some form of physical illness.

Jesus declared, "I am come that they might have life, and that they might have it more abundantly"

(John 10:10) and "Peace I leave with you, my peace I give unto you: not as the world giveth, give I unto you. Let not your heart be troubled, neither let it be afraid" (John 14:27).

Accept this gift of eternal life through Jesus Christ, our Lord. Jesus paid the price for our salvation by taking upon Himself the sins of us all. He suffered on our behalf because He loves us. Not only did he suffer for us, He shed His precious blood. Only the blood of Jesus Christ has the power to cleanse us from all our sins. Then Jesus paid the ultimate sacrifice of love: He died in our place on the cross so we might have eternal life.

Believe that Jesus is the Son of the Living God and that after three days He rose from the dead, alive in the flesh in His power. The resurrection is the only proof that Jesus was God Almighty Himself.

Confess or acknowledge that you have sinned and repent of your unbelief. Turn in faith to the One who can save you and take away the burden of sin. He will bring great peace and everlasting joy the moment you invite Him into your heart and life.

I do wish that every troubled or grieving person could experience such precious inner peace. I realized then, in the midst of mourning, I could have perfect peace. My prayer is that, as you read this God-inspired story, *The Legend of David's Amazing Harp*, you may sense the presence of

God's healing power and hear this beautiful, comforting music in your heart.

Will you take a moment right now and utter this prayer of faith? Invite the Comforter into your life today:

> *"Dear Lord, I acknowledge my need for the Comforter today. I confess my sins to You and ask for forgiveness. Come into my heart and change my life forever. Take away all my sins so I can go to heaven. Thank you, Lord God, for giving me a new life. Amen."*

Only Jesus can soothe, comfort, and bring healing to your soul.

The Shepherd is "our peace" Ephesians 2:14.

Take comfort now in Jesus' words from John 14:1,15 (TLB): "Let not your heart be troubled. You are trusting God, now trust in ME. If you love me, obey ME; and I will ask the Father and he will give you another Comforter, and he will never leave you" [emphasis mine].

My blessing to you is from Philippians 4:7: "And the peace of God, which passeth all understanding, shall keep your hearts and minds through Christ Jesus."

> *"Peace be within thy walls, and prosperity within thy palaces"* (Psalm 122:7).

"'COMFORT, YES, COMFORT my peo-ple,' says your God. 'Speak tenderly to Jerusalem and tell her that her sad days are gone. Her sins are pardoned...'" [and the Lord will give her twice as many blessings]'" (Isaiah 40:1–2 TLB, emphasis mine, paraphrased end).

"The SPIRIT of the Lord God is upon me, because the Lord has anointed me to bring good news to the suffering and afflicted. He has sent me to comfort the brokenhearted, to announce liberty to the captives, and to open the eyes of the blind. He has sent me to tell those who mourn that the time of God's favor to them has come, and the day of wrath to their enemies. To all who mourn in Is-rael He will give: beauty for ashes; joy instead of mourning; praise instead of heaviness" (Isaiah 61:1–3 TLB, empha-sis mine).

"The Lord will bless Israel again, and make her deserts blossom; her barren wilderness will become as beautiful as the Garden of Eden. Joy and gladness will be found there, thanksgiving and lovely songs" (Isaiah 51:3 TLB).

Only those who have put their trust in the Lord Jesus Christ and have experienced a change of life called the "New Birth" can enter heaven.

If you have truly accepted the Lord Jesus Christ into your heart and life, please write me and tell me about it.

Let My People Hear
P.O. Box 3021
Chattanooga, Tennessee 37404

Scan the code below to enjoy David's message on the "Is Your Name in the Lambs Book of Life?"

Obituaries

Dr. Donald E. Harrison

Dr. Donald E. Harrison was inducted into the Kingdom of God on December 16, 1999. The funeral service was conducted on December 20, 1999, by Rev. David Wood, his son-in-law, at the Riverview Baptist Church in West St. Paul, Minnesota.

Harrison was born in Mountain View, Minnesota, on July 10, 1936, after his twin brother, David M. Harrison. They grew up in South St. Paul.

Harrison got into trouble with a gang by breaking into a liquor store. The judge gave each member of the gang a choice to get involved with a church or join the Army.

He chose to drop out of high school and join the paratroopers. He served his time in Germany with his lifestyle as an unbeliever. While serving in Germany, an Army Chaplin, Merlin Carothers, a former bodyguard for General Dwight D. Eisenhower, came to the base to preach the gospel.

Hearing the Word of God over several nights, Donald came under great conviction and later surrendered his life by trusting Jesus Christ into his heart and life.

At that moment of faith, he took action by quitting smoking, changing his language, pouring all his liquor down the toilet, burning his pornographic magazines, making a public profession of his faith in Jesus Christ, and beginning to read the Bible.

God transformed his life by the power of the gospel to a new life in Jesus. After his release from the Army, he began attending college to prepare for the ministry. He graduated from Luther Rice Seminary with a Doctor of Ministry degree.

He taught at Liberty University in Lynchburg, Virginia, for seventeen years. Later he taught at Korea University in South Korea up to the time of his passing.

His twin brother David received the inspiration for The Legend of David's Amazing Harp while preparing to preach at his brother's funeral.

Catherine "Cathy" Hart Harrison

Catherine Hart "Cathy" Harrison, 82, of Chattanooga, Tennessee, departed this life for her heavenly home on Monday morning, November 7, 2022, at her home.

Cathy was born July 2, 1940, in Three Oaks, Michigan, a daughter of the late John Milton and Eunice May Phillips Brown. She was preceded in death by her brothers, John Brown, Robert "Bob" Brown, brother-in-law Donald E. Harrison (her husband's twin), father-in-law and mother-in-law, John Henry Harrison and Lois Harrison. She was deeply loved by all for her generosity and kind, gentle spirit.

Cathy was a 1958 graduate of Three Oaks High School, a graduate of Bethel College in St. Paul, Minnesota, and received her degree in nursing from Mounds-Midway School of Nursing in 1963. She was a registered nurse for fifty-nine years and was a Baptist by faith. Cathy wrote poetry and stories, read avidly, and collected stamps for over seventy years. She was a member of the River City Writer's Club and the Hearing Loss Association of America.

She is survived by her husband, Reverend David Harrison, and would have celebrated their 60th wedding anniversary on August 17, 2023; daughter and son-in-law, Doreen and Stephen H. Steele of Chattanooga, Tennessee; sons, Kevin David Harrison of Hanoi, Vietnam, and Nathan John Harrison of Tampa, Florida; daughter-in-law, Bethany Harrison of Palm Harbor, Florida; sister, Lois Hansen of Chelsea, Michigan; brothers- and sisters-in-law, Roy and Joan Brown of Three Oaks, Michigan, Richard "Dick" and Penny Brown of Bloomington Heights, Michigan, Mary Brown of Fennimore, Wisconsin, Marlene Key Ledo and Keith Harrison of St. Paul, Minnesota, and Susan Tillery of Mt. View, Missouri; grandchildren, Faith Steele, Grace Steele, Joy Steele, Maya Hart Harrison-Tang, Lily Grace Harrison-Tang, Isaac Harrison, Susanna Harrison, John Seb Harrison, and Cordelia Harrison; several nieces and nephews.

The family will receive friends at Ponders Brainerd Chapel, 4203 Brainerd Road, Chattanooga, on Sunday, November 13, from 1–3 pm. A service to celebrate the life of Mrs. Catherine "Cathy" Hart Harrison will be held at 3 pm with her husband, Rev. David Harrison, officiating. Music will be provided by Joe DePrimo and Nathan and Emily Garmany.

My Beloved Cathy:

On September 7, 2022, we celebrated our 59th anniversary at Niagara Falls, New York, while on a bus tour. It was the most exciting and happy time for both of us. Then you got sick on October 7 with congestive heart failure. After spending two days in two different emergency rooms, three days in the hospital, and eight days in the nursing home, you were finally released to come home on Saturday. You were promoted to heaven on Sunday, November 5, in your sleep.

I preached your funeral and shared the two greatest events in our lives. The first was when I accepted Jesus Christ into my heart on New Year's Eve 1958. You had already made a profession of faith when you were 11 years old while listening to Billy Graham on the radio.

The second greatest event was the day I walked unto the campus of Bethel College in St. Paul, Minnesota. We met the first day at a freshman retreat. You stole my heart, and you have been the love of my life ever since.

We talked a lot about heaven. I would always tell you, if you get there before I do, make sure that our mansion is on Gold Street and on the bank of the River of Life flowing from the throne of God. I miss you every day and look forward to our heavenly reunion.

Cathy and I on our wedding day, August 17, 1963.

ALBUM

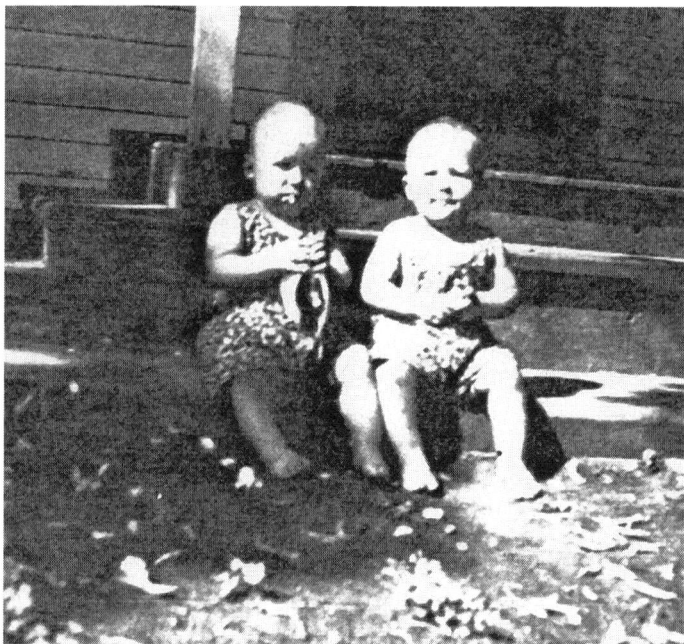

Don and I when we were about two years old
enjoying our bananas.

Don (right) and I outside our family home in South St. Paul, Minnesota.

Don (right) and I being caught in one of our many discussions.

My brother Don and sister-in-law, Ruth.

My brother Don (right) and I at my wedding in West St. Paul, Minnesota, August 17, 1963. He was my best man.

My brother Don and his wife Ruth on their wedding day, December 1963, Souix Falls, South Dakota.

My wife Kathy and I visiting our son K. David, in Philadelphia, Pennsylvania.